Thank You
Very Much

Thank You
Very Much

A book for anyone who has ever said,

"May I help you?"

Holly Stiel

Ten Speed Press
Berkeley, California

Ten Speed Press
P.O. Box 7123
Berkeley, California 94707
www.tenspeed.com

Distributed in Australia by Simon and Schuster
Australia, in Canada by Ten Speed Press Canada,
in New Zealand by Tandem Press, in South Africa
by Real Books, and in the United Kingdom and
Europe by Airlift Book Company.

Text and cover design by Ross Carron Design

First printing 1995

Printed in Canada

6 7 8 9 10 — 07 06 05 04 03

TO

You

A

SPECIAL

Thank You Very Much

TO

Alexander Zubak

Robert Spinrad

{ INTRODUCTION }

I worked at a busy desk in a large San Francisco hotel for over 16 years. On an average day we could have 300 guests come to us with a wide range of requests and seemingly endless questions.

Over the years of serving I always kept a little red notebook. This is where I would record my thoughts on the work I was doing. Eventually it became indispensable to me. I started writing in great quotes I heard, and even definitions of words so that I would know exactly what they meant. On days that weren't going too well, I'd flip through my little red book for inspiration, and I would always find it.

So, what I wanted to do was share my little red book, because there are so many of you out there who daily go through what I did for so many years.

This is your book now, not mine. Enjoy it!

Holly

Thank You Very Much

I don't know what your destiny will be,
But one thing I know:
The only ones among you
who will be really happy
are those
who
have sought and found
how to serve.

ALBERT SCHWEITZER

"Thank you very much."

These are the four most important words you can ever say, *or will ever hear.*

The first step

toward great

SERVICE is

WILLINGNESS

*WISDOM is ofttimes nearer
when we stoop than when we soar.*

WILLIAM WORDSWORTH

SERVE, (from Latin: *servire* = to serve)
To exert oneself continuously.
To render service so as to benefit,
    help, or promote.
To deliver in readiness.
To furnish or supply.
Synonyms: aid, advance, help, assist.

Remember who is in

C O N T R O L

Don't let the negative energy
of others attack you.

Never be angry
at your weaknesses.
As long as you acknowledge
them, you can work
on them.

That's the definition of

E X C E L L E N C E .

THE BUCK STOPS HERE:

When a customer asks you something,
it becomes YOUR responsibility.

CUSTOM, (from Latin: *consuescere* = to
accustom)
A habitual course of action; money,
service, etc., rendered by a feudal tenant
to his lord as due, also the obligation
to give custom. See also **CUSTOMER**.

THE CUSTOMERS
ARE ALWAYS RIGHT.

Even when they're wrong, they're right.

That's how it works.

In the real world there are
YES and **NO**.

In SERVICE there are
Yes and "May I suggest the following?"

BEFORE STARTING ANY SHIFT:

Take three deep breaths.

Say: "I can do this."

Quiet minds cannot be perplexed or frightened, but go on in fortune or misfortune at their own private pace, like a clock during a thunderstorm.

ROBERT LOUIS STEVENSON

> There is no sign above
> the entrance that tells the
> customers they have to be
> **WELL-MANNERED**

WHEN customers ask you for advice, find out about *them*.

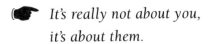 *It's really not about you, it's about them.*

ANTICIPATE, (from Latin *ante* = before + *capere* = to take)
To act before another; preclude or prevent by prior action, *as to anticipate a problem.*

If you ANTICIPATE a need, you won't have to solve a problem—and you'll save yourself a lot of stress, time, and energy.

Anticipate problems and
establish alternatives.

LIFE is pretty basic, so
customers will only rarely
surprise you. When they do,
thank them.

Style is HOW
you do something.

*It is a luxury
to be understood.*

RALPH WALDO EMERSON

"He was so rude, poor
soul. Thank goodness I
don't have *that* life!"

DEAD PEOPLE
DO THE **SAME** THING ALL THE TIME.
LIVING PEOPLE
DO **DIFFERENT** THINGS ALL THE TIME.
THAT'S THE DIFFERENCE.

[All service is
salesmanship.]

If you acknowledge
DISTRACTIONS you're wasting
your time, because distractions
are not important.

Some days are just horrible.

The cure is tomorrow.

The President *serves* his term.
We all *serve*.

IMAGINE THAT
Service
IS THE OLYMPICS:

Keep trying to break those
world records.

Recycle.

If you don't have a
recycling program at work,
offer to organize one.

(It will make you think about resources.)

Do one thing at a time.

Even if you have to do it quickly,
it should always be done

WELL.

At the end of every day,
ask yourself how you did
on a scale of one to ten.
And the result is
only for **you**.

Perception

IS YOUR CHOICE.

SERVICE IS
THE OPPORTUNITY TO
MAKE A DIFFERENCE IN
SOMEONE'S LIFE.

Even if you are dealing
with a customer for just a few minutes,
you are establishing a
r e l a t i o n s h i p .
(Relationships need to be *nurtured.*)

RELATIONSHIP, (from Latin: *referre* = to
bear together)
The state of being mutually interested.
Reverence or respect for another. To be
involved, concerned.

NURTURE, (from Latin: *nutrire* = to nurse)
To foster, educate, or nourish, as with food.

Don't be hard on yourself.

As long as you know that you want to learn and improve, you'll keep moving forward no matter what little failures you may have along the way.

Everybody uses the
FAVOR BANK.

But just like at a real bank, you have to make deposits before you can make withdrawals.

If your company has a

MISSION STATEMENT

memorize it.

*What really flatters someone is
that you think them worth flattering.*

GEORGE BERNARD SHAW

"Ed's okay. Like everyone, he has
his faults, but I like him anyway."
Customers are just like that.

**BEFORE A DIAMOND IS
CUT AND POLISHED, IT'S JUST A
LUMP OF ROCK.**

Given a choice between a
smiling person and one who is
frowning, who would
you approach?

If you are asked to STAY LATE
and you can, DO.

If you can't, EXPLAIN why and
DON'T FEEL GUILTY.

EXPERIMENT.

It's fun to see if you can make a grumpy
customer smile just by your shining example.

LEARN TO GET REINFORCEMENT

FROM YOUR WORK.

ORGANIZE, (from Greek: *organon* = that
with which one works)
To arrange or constitute in interdependent
parts, each having a special function or
relation with respect to the whole.

<u>Chance</u> works if you are a
casino.
If you aren't, get ORGANIZED.

Service is like what Mom
told you about piano lessons:

practice,
practice,
practice.

If a person tells you an idea that you just HATE, or that you know will turn out to be a DISASTER, nod positively and say:

"That's really interesting.
Tell me more about it."

A lot of bad ideas will just
SELF-DESTRUCT on examination,
and you won't be seen as
a negative person.

III

In every job there are THREE major things that need to be done. Make sure you clearly UNDERSTAND what those THREE things are in your job.

*H*osts are like generals:
it takes a mishap to reveal
their true genius.

HORACE

[
Everybody is somebody's friend.
How would you want *your* friends treated?
]

BE THE CAUSE OF WONDERFUL THINGS.

Service is one big game show: Always try
for the **BIG** prize!

Passion

is

energy

+

commitment.

PASSION, (from Latin: *pati* = to endure, suffer)

State or capacity of being affected by external agents or forces, strong emotion or feeling toward something, as in a *passion for accuracy.*

ENERGY, (from Greek: *ergon* = work)

Strength of expression; force of utterance; capacity of acting, power efficiently and forcibly exerted. *Synonyms:* strength, vigor, force.

COMMITMENT, (from Latin: *committere* = to connect)

A promise or pledge to do something.

Mistakes happen.

You are not perfect.
Acknowledge the mistakes,
say you're sorry, and
make amends.

Just BLOWING *is not playing
the flute: You must also use your fingers
and your brain.*

FREDERICK THE GREAT

EVERYBODY'S A MANAGER. WE ALL

MANAGE

TO GET THROUGH THE DAY.

Always know your resources.
If you'll just look around
you'll find plenty of help out there.
But you have to _look_.

Successful people know FEAR—
but *forge ahead* anyway.

Companies do not exist
for themselves. They exist for
(and because of) their

CUSTOMERS.

Don't forget this.

*A wise person will
make more opportunities
than seem to exist.*

SIR FRANCIS BACON

Two percent of
your customers won't be NICE.
Ninety eight percent will be.

What other business has such great odds?

Whenever possible
use the customers' **names**.
They love it.

GRACE, (from Latin: *gratus* = beloved)
Favor, kindness, mercy, virtue; esp. a
sense of right. Gracious, pleasing,
attractive, full of charm. *Synonyms:*
beneficent, friendly.

*The little unremembered acts
of kindness and love are the best
parts of a person's life.*

WILLIAM WORDSWORTH

It takes a
caring heart
and a sensible mind
to solve problems effectively.

SERVICE HAS THREE PARTS:

mental,

emotional,

physical.

AND IT'S LIKE A THREE-LEGGED STOOL:
which leg is the most important?

*Tell me to what you pay
attention and I will tell you
who you are.*

ALBERT EINSTEIN

The language of friendship is not words but **meanings**.

HENRY DAVID THOREAU

When a customer walks out
of your place of business
with a smile on their face—
THAT'S your product!

Make MEMORIES
for people through service.

*"Remember that wonderful person
at the hotel last year?"*

For any relationship to have a chance of success,
you must enter it in a positive frame of mind.
So, treat every customer as
if you were meeting a new friend.

SERVICE IS MEASURED BY

ACTIONS,

NOT BY

reputations.

Imagine that customers have
signs on them that say,

Make me feel
IMPORTANT!

S E L F - R E S P E C T

will always triumph over

disrespect.

RESPECT, (from Latin: *re* = again + *specere* =
to look)
To consider worthy of esteem; honor;
revere; venerate.

Be honest

when you can't handle something.
Excuse yourself and get help.

Before telling the boss anything,
take a moment to see it
from the boss's point of view.

$$\left\{ \begin{array}{c} \text{NEVER BE PETTY.} \\ \text{``SHE SAID THIS; HE SAID THAT,''} \\ \text{IS REALLY } \textit{boring.} \end{array} \right\}$$

*Speak when you are angry
and you will make the best speech
you will ever* REGRET.

AMBROSE BIERCE

Everything you do is important.
Everything.
And remember that *things*
aren't important.
ATTITUDE is.

A big part of *acting* is technique:
making people *believe* you are
the role you are playing.

A big part of *service* is technique:
making people *believe* you are
the role you are playing.

Service =

Technique + Attitude.

TECHNIQUE, (from Greek: *techne* =
      an art, artifice)
The method or details of procedure essential
to expertness of execution in any art or
science.

ATTITUDE, (from Latin: *aptus* = suited)
State of mind. Posture; position
assumed or studied to serve a purpose.

FOCUS, (from Latin: *focus* = the kitchen hearth or fireplace)
A central point or center of activity; adjustment to achieve distinct vision.

If it's out of your control,
don't waste time
worrying about it.
Focus on those things that
you CAN control.

Never be DEFENSIVE with a customer.
Never hide behind a counter or desk.
Never make excuses.
Only amateurs do that stuff.

Don't try to win in a disagreement
with a customer, because
being right is the booby prize.

{ THE BEST WAY TO REMAIN CALM IS TO
breathe deeply. }

When you do a great job,
ask yourself what it was that
made you so terrific.
Then REPRODUCE your answer.

S E R V I C E

What's your product?

The way the customers feel
after you've served them.

RHYTHM, (from Greek; *rhythmos* = measured
motion, from *rhein* = to flow)
Movement or action marked by regular and
predictable activity as in music, speech or dance.

Find the *rhythm* of your work each day.

Stay the same size all the time.

Some people will try to make you feel small.
Don't let them.

Every **BIG** thing

is made up of lots of little things. Mistakes happen

when we don't focus on each of the little things.

The SIMPLEST THINGS
are the most difficult,
so practice all the time.

There is no such thing as a pretty good omelet.

FRENCH PROVERB

Find something at work
that you just HATE doing, either
because you dislike it or are afraid
you won't do it well.
Then throw all your energy and
determination into that task.

It's a very liberating experience.

We never plan to fail,
but we often fail to plan.

*Many might go to heaven with
half the labor they use to go in precisely
the opposite direction.*

DR. JOHNSON

ENERGY.

YOUR PERSONAL ENERGY IS PRECIOUS.
USE IT WISELY.

Say to yourself:
"I'm really important."

Then turn to the person next to you and say:
"You're really important."

Then look at all the people in the room and say:
"You're all really important."

Finally say:
"Everyone's important."

IMPORTANT, (from Latin: *importare* =
to cause something to happen)
To have a high quality or meaning;
to be treated with special respect
and acknowledgment; to be of
consequence.

PRIDE, (from Anglo-Saxon: *pryte* = proud)
A reasonable delight in one's achievements;
self-respect and self-esteem.

When you do something well,
be proud.
You earned it.

A LL   SERVICE   IS

ACTING.

"It's that easy?"

"It's that easy."

Look at all the things you once
thought were impossible.
And now?
"That? **Nothing to it.**"

While you're struggling with
the FEAR that it can't be done,
somebody else is DOING IT.

"That customer made me so ANGRY!"
Only one person can control your anger:

You.

*The girl who can't dance always says the band
doesn't know how to play.*

MY MOTHER

Common courtesy,
LIKE COMMON SENSE, IS RARE.

{
Stay balanced.
Don't think only about work.
Make sure you have other interests.
}

Grooming

counts. Look the best you can.

Make sure you know
exactly what a customer is asking for:
CONFIRM and RECONFIRM.

THANK-YOU NOTES:

Anybody can write one.
Everybody loves getting one.

EFFORT, (from Latin: *ex* = from + *fortis* = strength)

Exertion of mental or physical power; a product of exertion, as a major effort.

A superstar *concentrates* just a little bit more than the ordinary player.

ALWAYS HAVE A CHEAT SHEET.
YOU CAN'T REMEMBER
everything.

CELEBRATE your successes
throughout the day.
(Mental pats on the back are always good.)

STRETCH.

Don't do the same thing the same way every day.
Stretch: try a different approach,
learn a new trick, add something to it.

STRETCH.

*No man is an island, entire of itself;
every man is a piece of the continent,
a part of the main.*

JOHN DONNE

PUNCTUALITY

is exactly the same at any job
you will ever have. If it's a problem for you,
then it has to be dealt with right *now*.

Always be at work
15 minutes early.

A *negative* COWORKER'S
a t t i t u d e
TELLS YOU MORE ABOUT THEM THAN THE SUBJECT
THEY THINK THEY'RE DISCUSSING.

If you work for a big company,
learn about its S T R U C T U R E .
It makes policies far more understandable.

The THIRD time a customer
comes in, you should address
him or her *by name.*

TAKE A LOOK AROUND REGULARLY.
A REAL, HARD, LONG LOOK.

*Goodness is the only
investment which never fails.*

HENRY DAVID THOREAU

When a customer asks for something, always ADD
one little thing to it: a smile, an added bit
of information, or something.
Or: *"I really hope you enjoy it."*

Nobody is ever born a great anything.

People learn and develop

S K I L L S .

SKILL, (from old Norse: *skil* = discernment)
The ability to use one's knowledge
effectively; a developed or acquired technical
proficiency.

People get bitten
by M O S Q U I T O E S , not elephants.

*It's the details and nuances
you need to watch carefully.*

BE PRACTICAL.

Learn skills.
Know your limits.

And then exceed them regularly.

If you are offered a company training class: GO.

Service
is a gift.

Don't become a victim of stress: DANCE through the day.

(And make your coworkers dance with you!)

Personal comments should
always be positive and general:

"You look great today!"

not *"I really love your figure."*

And bald people prefer that you not
point out the obvious, obviously.

The best answer to insults is silence.

SARAH BERNHARDT

Never lower your expectations.

ELIMINATE them altogether.
It makes the world a new and wonderful place.

EXPECTATION, (from Latin: *ex* =
out + *spectare* = to look for)
To wait for; mentally look for or expect;
look for as due or duty bound.

THE BEST STRESS RELIEVERS ARE:

m o v e m e n t

&

b r e a t h i n g .

(If you think you've got it BAD,
volunteer to serve meals
at a homeless shelter.
It is the fastest cure around.)

Don't let the daily rush
swamp you.
Stay in touch with yourself.

Never use formality
as a mask for **contempt**.
It will backlash on you every time.

*Besides, deep down it makes
you feel* **crummy**.

*Many forgive injuries,
but no one ever forgives contempt.*

Thomas Jefferson

The day before the boss gives you a

PERFORMANCE EVALUATION,

sit down and do one on yourself.
Then take it with you
to the meeting the next day.

OBSTACLES

are invitations for *creativity* and *skill*.

"THIS IS THE BEST I CAN DO."

Really?

You can't perhaps do 1 percent better,
and then 1 percent over that, etc.?
When you get to 110 percent, you can stop.

(But by then it's a habit.)

People

solve problems.
Technology only helps to make
the solutions faster.

CONVINCE, (from Latin: *convincere* = to conquer)
To bring by argument or action to belief beyond doubt.

Convince the *unhappiest* customer
in your day to be happy.

The best service in the world is
not necessarily flawless, but it is always

S I N C E R E .

Each day, consciously deal with one
situation that makes you UNCOMFORTABLE,
for whatever reason.
*Pretty soon you will have skills that
will make comfort a non-issue.*

If every customer were easy to
work with, you'd be BORED silly.
Difficult customers are the spice of life.
Enjoy them!

One of the beauties of
BEING POLITE
is that you are showing respect for the other person,
customer, or coworker. You can never go wrong
by being *sincerely* polite.

SINCERE, (from Latin: *sincerus* = undecayed)
Pure, unadulterated, honest. Without ulterior
motive.

Sometimes work is like being on AUTOPILOT.
Stop!

F E E L

what you are doing.

It takes more time to *complain*
than it takes to CHANGE.

W*e think in generalities,
but we live in details.*

LORD WHITEHEAD

{ Give customers what they want. }

Schmooze

is a great Yiddish word.
It means something like "buttering somebody up."
Customers love to be *schmoozed*.

Not just your *mouth*

S M I L E S :

your *eyes* and your *voice*
also need to smile.

Service is a *nurturing* profession.

Every morning, ask yourself:

"WHO'S DRIVING THIS BUS?"

Are you? *If not, that's the* FIRST
agenda item for the day.

You complain that the cards are ill shuffled until you get a good hand.

JONATHAN SWIFT

'Weakness' means:
"I haven't gotten around to PERFECTING
myself at that just yet."

TRUST ME:
Pampering your customers is
pampering yourself.

REWARD YOURSELF: a manicure,
an uninterrupted hour, a walk, whatever.

You deserve it.

(Bragging)
IS NEVER POPULAR OR APPRECIATED.

If you have *extra benefits* at work,
know exactly what they are.
You've EARNED them.

Customers never mind paying for
QUALITY or a valuable experience.
But if they think you're ripping
them off—*watch out!*

When someone says
they don't mind,
they mind.

AFRICAN-AMERICAN PROVERB

Always have a friend with whom you talk
about everything under the sun—

except work.

R EPETITION .

So much of our work is repetition.
But look closely: it's never *exactly* the
same with each customer.
Enjoy these little DIFFERENCES.

*One's best qualities
shouldn't be measured by
extraordinary circumstances,
but by everyday deeds.*

BENJAMIN FRANKLIN

A sense of HUMOR
is the most powerful weapon
against frustration.

► WELCOME TECHNOLOGY, AND USE IT. ◄

Indulge
customers.

They love that sort of thing.
(Besides, it's fun.)

No one is exempt from saying silly things. The mischief is saying them deliberately.

MICHEL EYQUEN DE MONTAIGNE

Only one person can keep a secret:

YOU.

Period, end of discussion.

Success comes in CANS.
I *can* do this.

(**FOCUS**)

*on what
you are doing.*

People who serve
aren't IMPORTANT.

Oh, yeah?

What if we didn't show up
for work one day?

The world would
stop.

*N*ever whisper to the deaf
or wink to the blind.

SLAVIC PROVERB

"What's *your* favorite?"

REALLY MEANS:

"What do you think
I will like?"

Think about what
customers are

hearing

from you.

O F F E R   S E R V I C E .
Don't wait to be asked.

Nothing was ever improved
by WORRYING about it.

Only put in the Suggestion Box things
that are phrased *positively*.

IF YOU ARE ON THE TIME CLOCK,

work.

ETHICS, (from Greek: *ethos* = custom, usage,
character)
The science of ideal human behavior and
character.

*It is impossible for
a person to be cheated by
anyone but themselves.*

OLD CHINESE PROVERB

Compliment yourself.

It's the best compliment you can get.
Don't wait for others to give it to you.

*Intelligence is finding
the extraordinary in others.*

PASCAL

EVOLVE, (from Latin: *evolvere* = to unroll)
A process of opening out what is contained
or implied in something. A development
leading to a definite end.

Innovate.

If the coffee maker should be over there,
work on getting it there.

Nothing is constant
except CHANGE.

Most people expect the
W O R S T
and are rarely disappointed.

NOBODY DOES SOMETHING
just FOR THE MONEY.

*No one does anything
from a single motive.*

AGATHA CHRISTIE

*It's a funny thing about life:
If you refuse to accept
anything but the best you
very often get it.*

W. SOMERSET MAUGHAM

☞ WHILE YOU'RE MAKING A LIVING,
DON'T FORGET TO LIVE.

SALARY, (from Old French: *salaire* = a pension
or stipend; from Latin: *sal* = salt)
Fixed compensation regularly paid for
services rendered.

{ Service pays a **psychic** salary:
It's really YOUR needs that
are being serviced. }

*We work not only
to produce, but to give
value to time.*

VINCENT VAN GOGH

DISCIPLINE, (from Latin: *discere* = a learner)
Training which molds, strengthens, or
perfects; rule or system of rules affecting
conduct or action.

'CHALLENGING' means

"Let's have fun doing something

we don't usually get to do."

Service isn't just getting from A to B.
It's *how* you get from A to B.

Every **BIG** success
is made up of lots of little *skills*.
The more skills you have, the

BIGGER

your *success* will be.

Look back and realize
how many times you have thought:
"I can't do this!"

But then you DID.

Amazing, huh?

IN SERVICE, a masterpiece
is a customer who arrives unhappy
and leaves happy.

But only an inspired and
disciplined artist can *create* a
MASTERPIECE.

{
RULE OF THUMB:

If you are not sure how to do something,
do it in the way you think will make the
customer feel absolutely terrific.
}

PROFESSIONAL, (from Latin: *pro* = strongly + *fateri* = to confess or say out loud)

Characteristic of or conforming to the standards of a profession; engaging in for livelihood or gain; engaged in by a professional as opposed to an amateur.

Your uniform should reflect your

PROFESSIONALISM,

not your personal taste.

A customer insults you, and you think:

"How dare you!"

As a PROFESSIONAL you

deal

with

the dare.

ENTHUSIASM, (from Greek: *en* = enter +
theos = the divine)
Great zeal or interest; to have tremendous
energy for; unstoppable.

*Nothing great was
ever achieved without
enthusiasm.*

RALPH WALDO EMERSON

Real customer service is
a strange blend of opposites:
REALISM & IDEALISM.

Do it for yourself.

*Don't do it for your mother
or the boss
or the company.*

Do it for *yourself*.

↑

THINK OF LIFE AS AN ELEVATOR:
YOU CHOOSE WHETHER TO PRESS "UP"
OR TO PRESS "DOWN."

↓

You can never know the moment
when you'll finally learn to do something.

That's why you always
have to *keep trying*.

Make sure you know the difference between
SERVICE and *servitude*.

Know your job description.

ESTEEM, (from Latin: *aestimare* = to value)
To appreciate the worth of; to hold in high
regard.

Self-esteem

is not a theory.
If YOU don't believe in yourself,
no one else can.

FRUSTRATE, (from Latin: *frustrare*= in vain)
To prevent from attaining a purpose; to bring
to nothing. *Synonyms*: thwart, block, outwit,
disappoint, circumvent.

FRUSTRATED,

UNHAPPY,

BORED?

Reinvent yourself.

Love does not consist in gazing at each other, but in looking together in the same direction.

ANTOINE DE SAINT-EXUPERY

🦆🦆🦆🦆🦆

Be organized.

(It's not as easy as it sounds.)

The other paycheck is

S E L F - E S T E E M .

(EVERYONE HAS WEAKNESSES.
WE JUST USE THEM DIFFERENTLY.)

Never assume.

Ask.

Find out for sure.

Practice eye contact
with customers.

There is nothing new
under the sun,
so don't reinvent the wheel.

LEARN.

ASK.

OBSERVE.

*If anyone is to remain pleased
with you, they should be pleased with
themselves when they think of you.*

BENJAMIN DISRAELI

If you *promise*, deliver.

PERIOD.

We *are much harder on people*
who betray us in small ways than
on people who betray others
in great ones.

SIR WALTER RALEIGH

Learn to read
body language.
The customer will tell you more with that
than with spoken language.

TRUE SERVICE COMES FROM THE *heart*.

CARING, (from Latin: *caritas* = to love)
Painstaking or watchful attention, heed,
or caution, as in *caring for children*.

Anything worth doing is worth doing *well*.

The relationship you have with
your customer starts with
the one you have with *yourself.*

Anyone who serves the public is in

PUBLIC   RELATIONS .

*Where the spirit
does not work with the hand
there is no art.*

LEONARDO DA VINCI

Be patient.

*He that has patience,
can have what he will.*

BENJAMIN FRANKLIN

IF SERVICE WERE *predictable,*

MACHINES COULD DO IT.

The MAIN EVENT at work isn't

the mechanical stuff you *have* to do.

It's serving people who happen

to be called customers.

YOU

do the job. The job doesn't do you.

Service is

EMOTIONAL.

If your feelings get hurt,
examine your feelings.

All service is

MULTIPLE-TASKED

(that's the fancy phrase for
I-gotta-do-sixty-things-at-once).
The way to survive is by
PRIORITIZING.
Then move down the list relentlessly.

AGGRAVATE, (from Latin: *aggravare* =
to make heavier, to make worse)

To make worse, more severe, more offensive;
to exasperate or irritate.

*"You know what
aggravates me to no end?
Customers who don't
know what they want!"*

Yes, it *is* like being Sherlock Holmes.
Sometimes you have to get to the mystery of:
What do they REALLY want?

"I don't know,"
is half the sentence.

The other half is,
"Let me find out for you."

Enjoy the DIFFERENCES (all of them)
of your customers.
As one coworker told me:

*"It's wild, it's crazy,
but it sure isn't boring!"*

Whatever you do,

L O O K

like you really know how to do it.

{ All service is personal. }

S HAKE HANDS
WITH CUSTOMERS.

*Vicious gossip is like
counterfeit money:
Many who wouldn't dream
of printing it have no qualms
in circulating it.*

OSCAR WILDE

It takes as much time and energy
to SHINE as it takes to whine.

With customers, as in life,

first impressions

are the most important.

As service people, we can **THINK**
whatever we want.
We simply can't **ACT** however we want.

*All that we are is a
result of what we have thought.*

GAUTAMA BUDDHA

How

will always reveal itself
if you use a nifty little trick called

thinking.

A waitress once said to me:
"It's all in how you look at it.
If you think POSITIVE, it will be.
Think negative and it is."
Wisest advice I ever got.

If you're not hearing

"THANK YOU VERY MUCH!"

then find out what it is
you're not doing.

DON'T DRIFT WITH THE TIDE.
Row.

A job well-done is
its own reward.
So reward *yourself*.

Think of *rhythm*

as dancing through your work.

{ FORGIVE yourself first

(*Then make it right.*) }

GLAMOUR, (from Scottish: var. of *grammar* in sense of *gramarge* = magic, enchantment)

Magic; quality of a person or place which engenders wonder or marvelous charm.

It's not the surroundings or the customers.

Only you can

make your job glamorous.

DO NOT DATE YOUR COWORKERS.

(We all know why, right?)

Love your neighbor, but don't pull down the fence.

SWISS PROVERB

You do not have to be every coworker's friend, but you should be aware of how you are PERCEIVED. If you don't like the perception, *change it.*

No one ever achieved anything without pursuing it first.

Job security has nothing to do
with the job you have right NOW.
It's the skills of your profession
and how well you use them.

To be in hell is to drift.
To be in heaven is to steer.

GEORGE BERNARD SHAW

How do you recognize great service?

By what the person DID,
not by what they SAID they'd do.

> "Well, what is going to make the
> customers happy, anyway?"
> Try the direct approach:
>
> ASK THEM.

Don't ask the doctor;
ask the patient.

ITALIAN PROVERB

Get good TOOLS.

If you walk a lot, get good shoes.
If the phone's your tool, get a headset.
If you talk a lot, drink water regularly.

*Tact is the intelligence
of the heart.*

EMILY POST

Nobody ever forgets
where they buried the hatchet.

AFRICAN-AMERICAN PROVERB

{ Go with the flow. }

LEARN FROM EVERYBODY.

Remember:
There is somebody smarter
than all of us and that is:
everybody!

NAPOLEON BONAPARTE

Service never judges.

LEARN SOMETHING

N E W

ABOUT YOUR JOB EVERY WEEK.

*It is useless to close
your door to new ideas, they'll
come in through the window
and down the chimney.*

COUNT METTERNICH

EDUCATION, (from Latin *ex* = out + *ducere* = to lead)
Discipline of mind or character through study or instruction. *Synonyms:* training, discipline, breeding.

Teach your coworkers
what you know.
It makes your job and
your life a lot
E A S I E R .

No one has EVER had these dying words:
"I think I learned too much."

Shout long enough that you are right and you will be wrong.

HAWAIIAN PROVERB

If you learn mountain climbing,
molehills will be a piece of cake.

The best teaching method is
EXAMPLE.

Life without weaknesses
would be boring.

What would we be working on?

WHEN SOMEBODY SAYS:

"Oh, you couldn't possibly do that,"

THINK OF IT AS AN

engraved invitation.

Don't waste your precious energy
on silly stuff like *anger, hate, depression,
fear,* or *vindictiveness.*
Use energy WISELY and to your BENEFIT.

PANIC, (from the Greek god Pan who was
supposed to cause sudden and
inexplicable terror and surprise)
An immediate and overpowering fright of
a groundless nature.

Panic is losing control.

D e e p   b r e a t h .

Then, start with the closest thing at hand and
re-establish control, one thing at a time.

Remember

to

BREATHE.

ASPIRE, (from Latin: *aspirare* = to breathe upon)
To seek to attain something. To desire eagerly.

INSPIRE, (from Latin: *in* + *aspirare* = to breathe into)
To affect so as to enliven, animate, and fill with energy. To make enthusiastic.

If you work with the public,

U S E

B R E A T H   M I N T S .

Be self-reliant.

*Give yourself the satisfaction of
figuring it out on your own.*

$\Big($ Never give up.

Never.

You *can* do it. $\Big)$

MOTIVATION, (from Latin: *movere* = to move)
That within the individual, rather than without, which incites him to action.
Synonyms: inducement, incentive, impulse.

CHALLENGE YOURSELF WITH YOUR WORK EVERY DAY.

We can do anything we want to if we stick to it long enough.

HELEN KELLER

Keep my words positive:
Words become my behaviors.
Keep my behaviors positive:
Behaviors become my habits.
Keep my habits positive:
Habits become my values.
Keep my values positive:
Values become my destiny.
There is no dress rehearsal:
This is one day in YOUR *life.*

MAHATMA GANDHI

THE GOLDEN RULE

Do unto others
as you would have them
do unto you.

Your face is the TV screen.

Your *attitudes* and *moods* are the shows.

ALL THE WORLD'S A STAGE.

Know your part.

I used to have

stage fright.

Then one night, as I was waiting
to go on, I thought:
*"If I spent half the energy on acting
that I'm spending on worrying,
I might be halfway decent."*

I never had stage fright again.

All service deals with

P E O P L E ,

not things. We may be selling things,
but it is people who hand over the money for them.

P   E   O   P   L   E   .

Great service isn't the stuff on the outside.

It's the stuff on the *inside*.

Look F E A R *in the face.*

Fear is like fog.

Shine a warm light on it and it vanishes.

Do nothing, and you won't

be able to see a thing.

"That customer hurt my feelings,"

REALLY MEANS,

*"I **let** that customer hurt my feelings."*

Don't just plod through the day.

D   A   N   C   E   !

With each customer, say to yourself:
"We're both going to be winners!"

EFFECTIVE, (from Latin: *ex* = out +
        facere = to make)
Producing a decided, decisive, or desired
effect; efficient. Ready for service; also
impressive or striking, as in *an effective style.*

Money is a NECESSITY, a means to live.
It is not a goal.
If money is your goal, then you don't have one.

Getting fired is always traumatic.
It is not, however, the end of the world.

D e e p   b r e a t h . . .

RECREATION, (from Latin: *re* = again +
creare = to create)
A re-creating; refreshment of strength after toil;
diversion or play.

You're not immortal or invincible. Take time to
RECHARGE YOUR BATTERIES every day.

At the end of each workday, take a moment
to *celebrate* your favorite customer.

When you take a break, *really* take a break.

Don't think about work.

RELAX, (from Latin: *re* = again + *laxare* = loosen)
To make less firm, rigid, or tense; to make
less severe or strict.

Do you regularly miss a night's sleep?
Then also make sure you consciously do
something good for yourself every day.

*Experience is not what
happens to a person. It is what
that person does with what
happens to them.*

ALDOUS HUXLEY

"I didn't mean
to be nasty.

I just forgot to
be *nice*."

Some customers just want to
COMPLAIN.
They will always find a reason.
Anything will do.
That's part of the job.

Nothing will tell you more about yourself than the way you act toward fools.

MARK TWAIN

Every complex process
is made up of parts.
Break it down to those parts
and deal with each

i n d i v i d u a l l y .

Irate customers are a lot like MT. EVEREST:
If you just ignore them, will they vanish?

I slept and dreamt that life was joy.

I woke and realized that life was

S E R V I C E .

I acted, and behold

Through service there was joy.

INDIGENOUS AMERICAN PROVERB